TAHA

How A Prostitute Saved The World's Top Fashion And Clothing Company

VISHAL GUPTA

Grab your Free Gift

As an act of appreciation and gratitude, I would like to offer you a **FREE GIFT**:

Click below to download a free copy of my book **"TOXIC PEOPLE."**

This book has transformed the lives of thousands worldwide, and I am sure it will also be helpful to you.

So, what are you waiting for?

GRAB YOUR FREE COPY BY CLICKING ON THE LINK BELOW:

http://vishal-gupta.com/freebook

TABLE OF CONTENTS

4   Authors Note

6   Introduction

7   The Falling Empire

11   The Escape

15   Midnight Encounter

20   Taha's Unconventional Wisdom

31   Returning to his Empire

44   Battling Scepticism

51   A Resurgence of Hope

55   Taha's Second Lesson

59   The Offer

63   From the Streets to the Boardroo

70   Embracing Change

74   A Union of Minds

78   The New Dawn

82   Love Beyond Boundaries

85   Shaping minds

88   Marriage

91   Movement

94   Your Ratings and Review Matter

95   Acknowledgments

95   Dedication

96   Disclaimer

Authors Note

Who am I to pen down words about prostitutes and their unacknowledged genius? What endows me with the authority or credibility to address such a delicate subject?

As a criminal lawyer, I found myself representing prostitutes under India's Prevention of Immoral Trafficking Act (PITA). This professional proximity allowed me a glimpse into their lives and experiences. Through our regular interactions, I discerned that many of these women, despite being products of unfortunate circumstances, were not only astute but also compassionate, emotional, and profoundly human. Society is often hasty in its judgment, failing to see beyond labels and recognize the true essence of an individual. It was during these engagements that I resolved to one day write about them – to paint a picture not just of their struggles, but also of their resilience, intelligence, and beauty.

This book stands as a homage to the countless commercial sex workers ostracized by society through no fault of their own. I hope it offers a new lens through which readers can view and appreciate these remarkable individuals.

Dear readers, "Genius can be found in the most unexpected of places, in the most unexpected of minds. It is often glimpsed in the shadows, overshadowed by societal judgments and prejudices. But when it emerges, it shines so brightly that it cannot be ignored. In the world of marketing, there exists an unsung hero, an individual who possesses an innate understanding of human desires and the art of persuasion. This person, whom many overlook and dismiss, is called by many names-a prostitute, a commercial sex worker, an escort, a woman of the night.

I know what you must be thinking - how can a prostitute, someone whose profession is enveloped in societal stigma, possess the brilliance and insight needed to transform a struggling business? Yet, the reality is that a Prostitute understands the nuances of customer satisfaction, of creating ecstasy amidst the storm of rejection. They possess a tenacity and resourcefulness that can breathe life into even the most ailing business. The most brilliant marketing minds do not necessarily reside in ivory towers or prestigious institutions. Instead, they wear the cloak of anonymity, often shunned by society, their brilliance simmering beneath the surface.

In 'Taha,' I invite you to delve into a world where preconceptions and biases are shattered, where unlikely heroes rise above the noise to rewrite the rules of success. Through this extraordinary tale, I hope to challenge the traditional notions of brilliance, to inspire you to seek the extraordinary in the ordinary, and to understand that the best marketing minds are not always where you expect them to be.

So, join me on this captivating journey as we unravel the secrets of marketing, where a prostitute's wisdom illuminates the path to success. In the end, you may find yourself questioning your own definitions of genius and realizing that sometimes, it's the most unexpected minds that hold the power to change the world."

INTRODUCTION

This story is about the journey of two completely different individuals from completely diverse background having absolutely nothing in common expect the will and courage to go beyond preconceived notions, society biases, traditional ideas and to seek inspiration in the most unexpected places.

It's a story of the meeting of two extra-ordinary minds who collaborate to innovate, grow, and transform. It's a story of love, hope, success amid adversity, chaos and scepticism.

This book will take the readers on a rollercoaster of emotions, business strategies, and profound realizations. It delves into the world of fashion and the heart of human psychology, asserting that true genius doesn't always reside in boardrooms or ivy-covered halls. Sometimes, it's found in the quiet corners of society, waiting to be recognized. Dive in, as George and Taha redefine the world of fashion marketing, offering a fresh perspective and reminding us that innovation, inspiration, and love can blossom in the most unexpected terrains.

A tale of two worlds, two lives, intertwined by fate.

THE FALLING EMPIRE

George Miller's rise had been nothing short of meteoric. He was the embodiment of the global fashion empire, with shimmering showrooms that sparkled in the poshest streets from Paris to Tokyo. These palaces of luxury, teeming with the latest couture, had become synonymous with style, elegance, and aspiration. Yet, as George Miller strode into the opulent boardroom, his sharp gaze scanning the room filled with his top executives. The mood was somber, as the projection screen displayed the declining sales graphs and sinking profit margins. George's heart sank. The once-thriving company was now bleeding from all corners.

Months of strategy sessions, market research, and campaigns had yielded no significant improvement. Every attempt to revive the brand met with more resistance, and morale was at an all-time low. The eyes of his employees, once filled with pride and ambition, now showed traces of despair.

A sense of unease gripped George's heart. The weight of hundreds of showrooms, thousands of employees, and countless dreams that relied on his leadership bore down on him. The numbers didn't lie; sales had been declining for the past few years. His once mighty empire, which stood tall against industry storms, now seemed on the brink of a collapse.

"What are we missing?" George mused aloud, addressing his marketing head, Martin, a Harvard Business School prodigy. Martin, usually so eloquent, struggled for words. The rest of the room was equally silent.

His highly-skilled marketing team, composed of graduates from the finest institutions, seemed to be losing touch. Their strategies, once groundbreaking, now failed to resonate with their target audience. The world had changed, and George's empire was not adapting fast enough.

In the distance, George's secretary whispered, passing a note. It was another piece of bad news — a leading fashion magazine had just published a scathing review of their latest collection. George felt as if the universe conspired against him.

He reminisced about the early days, the tireless nights, the sheer passion, and drive that had gone into building the brand. The memories of his father handing over the reins of a budding business, trusting young George's vision, played before his eyes. "Take it forward, son," his father's voice echoed. "Make it touch the skies." And he had.

However, the fashion landscape had shifted. Trends were no longer just about the fabric or the design. They were intertwined with stories, personal narratives, and authenticity. Digital disruption had given rise to indie brands that connected with the youth, leveraging social media platforms to narrate relatable stories. These new-age brands spoke the language of the streets, of rebellion, of activism, and of identity.

George's empire, in contrast, had remained ensconced in its golden bubble of haute couture. It represented an old-world charm that, while exquisite, felt distant from the beating heart of the young and restless. Their marketing campaigns, though glossy and high-budget, lacked the soul that resonated with new consumers.

As he sat at the head of the long rectangular table in the boardroom, the tension was palpable. Concerned glances were exchanged, whispers hushed. The meeting commenced with the CFO presenting the bleak financials. There were mentions of cost-cutting, possible layoffs, shutting down less profitable outlets, but George's mind seemed distant.

Looking around, he realized that many at that table had never stepped out of the boardroom's confines to feel the pulse of the real market. Their perspectives were shaped by data points, bar graphs, and pie charts. While these were essential, the soul of fashion - the rhythm, the narrative, the connection - seemed amiss.

Linda, from the marketing department, passionately presented a new campaign proposal. It showcased supermodels against exotic locales, a symphony of luxury. However, George felt an unsettling hollowness. "Is this us?" he pondered. "Are we merely about showcasing unattainable dreams? What about the real dreams, the everyday aspirations?"

After hours of discussions, as the board members filed out, George felt an overwhelming sense of isolation. As he stared out of his corner office window, the bustling city below seemed so distant. It was a world that was moving on, evolving, and somehow, he felt left behind.

Every fiber of George's being felt weary. The gravity of his empire's troubles, the sinking feeling of being the captain of a drowning ship, had become a tormenting specter that haunted him day and night. His once sharp and analytical mind now felt like a maze of confusion. The whispers of doubt were louder than ever, questioning every decision he had made, the paths he had chosen, and the future he had envisioned for the company.

He could no longer recognize his reflection in the mirror—those intense eyes that once bore dreams and determination now reflected a hollow, defeated man. George's golden touch, which had transformed every project into a roaring success, felt lost. The allure of his grand office, the intoxicating power it held, now felt suffocating. It was a constant reminder of his inadequacies and failures.

THE ESCAPE

One evening, as the sun cast a fiery hue over the city, drowning it in golden and amber tones, George found himself at his penthouse balcony. He gazed into the horizon, the chaotic buzz of the metropolis below contrasting starkly with the silent chaos in his heart.

Desperation whispered to him, "Escape. Find solace. Rediscover yourself."

And thus, the idea of a getaway took root. He didn't want a meticulously planned vacation, with luxury suites and itineraries. He wanted an escape, an unplanned journey to a place where no one knew George Miller, the magnate. He wanted to be just George, a man seeking answers.

As George packed his bags to an undisclosed location, he realized that sometimes, to rebuild, one must first crumble. The 'Falling Empire' wasn't just about dwindling sales; it was about lost narratives, forgotten stories, and a disconnect with an evolving world. The revival would require more than just new designs; it demanded a new soul.

Before dawn, with just a backpack, George sneaked out of his penthouse, avoiding the ever-watchful eyes of the media and his overzealous staff. He didn't inform anyone, not even his closest confidants. He drove his car, a sleek black machine that had always been more of a symbol of his status than a mode of transport, to the city outskirts, then ditched it for an old rental, ensuring his movements would remain discreet.

He headed west without a destination in mind. The open road, with its endless stretches and changing landscapes, seemed therapeutic. The luxury of solitude gave him time to introspect, and the raw, untouched beauty of nature began chipping away at the walls around his heart.

George's disappearance was met with shockwaves across the industry. The media buzzed with speculations, competitors anticipated the company's downfall, and employees feared an uncertain future. Yet, for George, this break was a quest - a quest for answers, for revival, and for rediscovering the soul of his brand.

Days turned into nights and nights into days as George drove through sleepy towns and expansive meadows, stopping at local diners and motels. The anonymity of these places, where people were strangers with their stories, was a balm to his bruised soul.

In a quaint town nestled between hills, George's journey took an unexpected turn. While sipping coffee at a roadside cafe, he overheard locals talking about a week-long festival in a neighboring village, celebrating life, nature, and stories. Intrigued, George decided to head there, hoping the festivity might offer a diversion from his consuming thoughts.

The village was a picture of rustic charm. Cobblestone streets, houses adorned with flowers, and the ever-present sound of laughter painted a scene straight out of a storybook. The festival, it turned out, was an age-old tradition where people from all walks of life shared tales— of love, loss, hope, and dreams.

That evening, as George sat among the villagers, listening to a fisherman narrate his encounter with a mermaid or a young girl talking about her dream of touching the stars, he felt a connection. These were not just stories; they were raw emotions, dreams, and experiences that bridged the gap between reality and fantasy.

One evening, a woman named Mia shared her tale of finding love in the most unexpected place, at a time when she had given up all hope. Her story, filled with twists, passion, and raw emotion, resonated deeply with George. It made him ponder love's unpredictable nature and how it could be the key to finding oneself.

As days melded into one another, George found himself immersed in the village's life. He helped set up stalls, participated in dance rituals, and even shared his story— one of dreams, success, loss, and the search for meaning. The villagers, unaware of his real identity, welcomed him as one of their own.

However, as the festival's end neared, the weight of his responsibilities began to resurface. George realized he couldn't run forever. The empire, the employees, the legacy—everything awaited his return.

Yet, this getaway had not been in vain. The village and its stories had given him something invaluable—a fresh perspective. The realization dawned that perhaps the solution to his problems didn't lie in boardroom strategies or marketing gimmicks but in reconnecting with the human spirit, the stories, and the emotions that drive them.

With a heavy heart and a promise to return, George left the village. But he carried with him the memories, the lessons, and a newfound hope that he could rebuild his empire, not just with brick and mortar, but with stories, passion, and a genuine connection with people.

Midnight Encounter

The city lights glistened under the velvet canopy of the night sky. The streets, bathed in a soft luminescent glow, pulsed with the energy of nocturnal life. Bars, cafes, and late-night diners painted a tableau of urban allure and mystery. The city, like an enchantress, beckoned with her many secrets, waiting to be discovered.

George, returning from the rejuvenating trip to the village, felt out of place amidst the city's glamour and chaos. The juxtaposition of his recent experiences in a quaint village and this overwhelming urban life was jarring. He found himself missing the simplicity and warmth of the village folk and their heartwarming stories.

With each step on the concrete pavement, memories of the village festival flashed before him — the joyous dances, the shared laughter, the poignant stories. It felt like an entirely different world, one that seemed much more real and connected than this concrete jungle.

Feeling the weight of his own solitude, George decided to take a long walk to clear his mind before heading to his home. The streets, usually bustling with activity during the day, revealed another side of the city at night.

It was past midnight when George wandered into a dimly lit alley, the sounds of the main street fading with each step. The alley led to a quaint square lined with old buildings, their history etched in their stone facades. In the center was a fountain, its gentle trickling sound providing a serene backdrop.

Walking aimlessly through the winding streets, he bumped into a striking women, her eyes radiating a unique combination of mystery and warmth, as they exchanged apologies, there was a momentary pause, a silent acknowledgement of a connection neither had anticipated. The woman introduced herself as Taha, a woman of the night. This first encounter was far from a fairy-tale meet-cute. He was seeking distraction, while she was just looking for her next client. Driven by loneliness and a need for temporary escape, George decided to engage Taha's services and checked into a hotel.

However, when they reached the hotel room, the usual transactional nature of Taha's work hit a wall. George's worries made him distant, lost in his thoughts, leaving no space for physical intimacy. Sensing his discomfort, Taha inquired about the cause of his distress.

Reluctantly, George opened up, narrating the downfall of his empire. Taha, surprisingly, was familiar with his brand. She listened intently, her eyes reflecting genuine interest. And as the night progressed, George would learn that beneath Taha's street-smart demeanor was a mind brimming with untapped insights and strategies.

The room's ambient lighting cast a warm glow over the spacious hotel room, making the modern decor seem all the more inviting. But neither of the room's occupants seemed particularly interested in the aesthetics. Instead, they were both lost in the magnitude of the moment, with George looking out the window pensively and Taha seated comfortably on the bed.

"Taha," George began, taking a deep breath. "I've opened up to you tonight in a way I haven't with anyone in a long while. I'm managing an empire that's slipping through my fingers, and it feels suffocating."

Taha shifted her position, drawing her knees up to her chest. "You know, George," she began, her voice soft but assured, "my world is very different from yours. Every night, I step out onto the streets, and it's like entering a battlefield. But it's also my marketplace. To survive, I've had to become an expert in understanding people, in marketing, in a sense. Not the kind you learn in business schools, but the raw, unfiltered kind."

George looked at her, intrigued. "Go on."

She continued, "Every client is different. Some are searching for intimacy, some for escapism, and others, just a listening ear. My livelihood depends on reading these signals correctly, understanding their desires, and positioning myself accordingly."

There was a pause, the gravity of her revelation sinking in. George's initial surprise slowly morphed into curiosity. "How do you do it? How do you decode a person so quickly?"

Taha smiled wryly. "It's a blend of intuition, observation, and experience. For example, just like you have trends in fashion, we have trends on the streets. And I need to stay ahead of these trends, be it in the way I present myself or the services I offer."

George leaned forward, captivated. "But how does that relate to my world, to the world of fashion?"

Taha replied, "It's about being in touch with your customer, truly understanding them. Maybe your marketing team, with all their degrees and expertise, is missing this basic human connection. Perhaps they're too removed from the streets, from the real world. They've forgotten how to listen and observe."

Taha spoke of a childhood marked by hardship and resilience, of dreams that were bigger than her circumstances, and the choices she made, both willingly and out of necessity. She told him of the world that judged her for her profession, but also of the countless souls she'd met, each carrying their own burdens and secrets.

George, listening intently, was captivated not just by her story, but by the way she told it—with raw honesty and a lack of self-pity. For someone who had faced such adversities, her strength was evident in every word she spoke, in every emotion she conveyed.

Taha's tales from her profession intrigued George the most. She shared insights on human behavior, on desires, insecurities, and the masks people wore. "In my line of work," she began with a wistful smile, "I've learned that everyone has a story. And often, it's the unspoken words, the subtle gestures, that reveal the most."

She spoke of how she tailored her approach to every client, understanding their needs and desires, not just physically, but emotionally and psychologically. "Marketing oneself is a complex game," she mused. "It's about reading people, anticipating their wants, and offering them an experience that stays with them long after the night is over."

The hours flew by, and as the first rays of dawn approached, George felt a weight lifting off his shoulders. In Taha, he had found an unexpected confidante, someone who viewed the world from a perspective he had never considered.

As they left the lounge, the early morning breeze carrying the scent of the sea, George realized that this encounter, though accidental, might just be the catalyst he needed to redefine his empire. Taha's unconventional wisdom, born out of her unique life experiences, had given him more clarity in one night than months of board meetings and consultations had.

Walking Taha to her home, they promised to meet again, both aware that their paths crossing wasn't just a fleeting connection, but the beginning of a transformative journey for both of them.

TAHA'S UNCONVENTIONAL WISDOM

The sun had risen, heralding a new day in the city. Yet for George, the events of the previous night seemed like an ethereal dream, almost too poignant to be true. Sitting on the plush bed of his luxurious apartment, he played back the conversation with Taha. The striking contrast of their backgrounds, her raw insights, the depths of her soul, and her unconventional wisdom. It all seemed too overwhelming, too beautiful.

A single encounter had broadened George's perspective immensely. Taha, a woman of the night and a woman society deemed unworthy, had showcased a wisdom that was unmatched by even the most learned in his circle.

As George delved deeper into their conversation, he realized that the core of Taha's insights centered around one primary fact: the understanding of human emotions and desires. It wasn't about flashy advertising or aggressive sales tactics; it was about connecting with the customer on a deeply personal level, resonating with their emotions, their hopes, their aspirations.

Tahas' beauty and intelligence captivated George. He'd never encountered a woman like her before. Taha was important to him, and he knew she had more to offer. Nothing happens by chance, George reasoned. The universe is constantly sending signals and messages through individuals. He realized that Taha was a divine message for him. He suggested another meeting with her. He promised Taha her professional compensation for the meeting, ensuring that she was adequately valued for her time and services.

Taha began by explaining the essence of her world. "In my line of work," she had said, her voice soft, yet firm, "We don't have the luxury of false advertising. No branded campaigns, no celebrity endorsements. It's just me, my body, and the audience. And every single time, I have but a few moments to connect, to make them feel something, to ensure they see my worth."

"Human touch and human connect is important," she whispered.

George thought about this. His fashion empire had been built on glitz and glamour, on showcasing a life of luxury that everyone aspired to. But somewhere down the line, they had lost the human touch. It had become less about how the clothes made one feel and more about the image it projected.

Taha's next insight was even more profound. She spoke about vulnerability. "When I stand there on the streets, I am vulnerable. But it's this very vulnerability that draws people in. They see the raw, unfiltered me, and it resonates with them." She looked deeply into George's eyes. "Tell me, George, when was the last time your brand was vulnerable?

When was the last time you showcased not just the perfect, glamorous life but the struggles, the little moments, the stories that make us all human?"

This struck a chord with George. In the world of fashion, everything was about perfection. The perfect body, the perfect lifestyle, the perfect image. But real life was messy, filled with ups and downs, and it was in these imperfections that true beauty lay.

Taha went on, her voice a gentle caress, guiding George through a labyrinth of insights. "Marketing, at its core, is about stories. And every person has a story. A story that's waiting to be heard, to be seen. Your job is not to sell clothes. It's to tell these stories, to be a part of them."

She painted a vivid picture, drawing from her life's experiences. From the stories of the people she met on the streets every night, from the hopes and dreams of the street food vendor who gives her food everyday, to the elderly man who saw his lost love in her eyes.

"Every night," Taha said, her voice filled with emotion, "I sell dreams, memories, emotions. I don't have a fixed price. People pay what they feel. And believe me, when you touch someone's soul, when you become a part of their story, they see your worth."

She further explained, "In my line of work, reputation is everything. Word of mouth can make or break you. Similarly, in the fashion world, you need your customers to be your biggest advocates. It's not just about creating clothing; it's about creating an experience."

Stretching out her arms and taking a deep breath, Taha said, "You see, George, your world isn't too different from mine. At its core, marketing, whether it's for a high-end brand or a night on the streets, is about fulfilling desires, creating connections, and selling dreams."

As she spoke, Taha began outlining her approach, breaking it down into digestible chunks. It was like watching a master at work, her concepts weaving seamlessly into a cohesive whole.

1. Personalized Experience: "Every client is unique. What they seek, their desires, their fears – I tailor my approach based on these nuances. Similarly, for your brand, every customer should feel special, seen, and catered to."

2. The Power of Storytelling: "It's not just about the service; it's about the narrative. Each of us carries a story, a history. Share the stories of the artisans who craft your clothes, the legacy of your brand. Make it immersive."

3. Create Genuine Connections: "Authenticity is key. Whether it's a genuine compliment or a shared secret, real connections create lasting impressions. Your brand should strive for that same authentic connection."

4. Understand and Anticipate Needs: "Often, clients themselves aren't fully aware of what they seek. It's about reading the unspoken, feeling the pulse of the room. Similarly, your brand should be two steps ahead, anticipating fashion needs even before they become trends."

5. Embrace Vulnerabilities: "Nobody's perfect. Sometimes, vulnerabilities become assets when

presented rightly. Perhaps, there are aspects of your brand, production imperfections or past mistakes. Embrace them, make them part of your narrative."

6. Diversify and Innovate: "Variety is the spice of life. New experiences, different settings—it keeps things fresh. Your collections, events, showrooms should have that element of surprise, that touch of the unexpected."

As she wound up her pitch, there was a charged silence. The juxtaposition of Taha's unconventional wisdom against the backdrop of George's high-fashion empire was both startling and enlightening.

Throughout the day, George made notes, seeing clear parallels between Taha's strategies and potential innovations for his brand. From creating personalized shopping experiences to fostering genuine connections through storytelling and brand authenticity, Taha's insights were gold.

George was spellbound. Here was a woman who had faced unimaginable adversities, who society looked down upon, and yet her understanding of human psyche, of marketing, was profound. She didn't have a degree from a prestigious institution, but her life had been her teacher.

She concluded with a powerful statement. "In a world that's increasingly becoming disconnected, where screens have replaced human touch, where algorithms decide what we see, it's more crucial than ever to reconnect. To go back to basics. To understand that at the end of the day, we are all humans, craving connection, love, and understanding."

As the sun streamed through the windows, George felt a weight lifting off his shoulders. Taha's unconventional wisdom had shown him the path. He felt invigorated, ready to take on the challenges, to bring his empire back from the brink, not with flashy campaigns but with heart, with stories, with connection.

He realized that the essence of marketing, of life, was not in the grand gestures but in the little moments, in the stories that make us human. And as he looked out of the window, he sent out a silent thank you to Taha, the woman who had changed his life with her unconventional wisdom.

As the days flowed into nights, George found himself spending more time with Taha. Every interaction was an exploration, a journey into the depths of human psyche, desires, and ambitions. Each evening, they'd pick a new location in the town—a quiet coffee shop, a bustling market square, or the tranquil beach—and dive deep into conversations. Every beautiful location added to the intensity of their conversation.

One evening they met at the "Café Luminara," a coffee shop known for its intimate ambiance and artisan brews. From the outside, Café Luminara was an enchanting sight. Its facade was adorned with creeping ivy and a vintage signboard that swung lightly with the breeze. Soft golden light streamed out from its large windows, inviting passersby into its warm embrace.

As George pushed open the vintage wooden door, a gentle bell jingled overhead. The scent that greeted them was an intoxicating blend of freshly roasted coffee beans, aged wood, and the faintest hint of vanilla.

The interior of Café Luminara was a harmonious blend of rustic charm and modern elegance. Exposed brick walls provided a warm, earthy backdrop, upon which hung an eclectic mix of artwork—oil paintings of landscapes juxtaposed with contemporary abstract pieces. Wooden beams crisscrossed the ceiling, from which hung vintage chandeliers that cast a soft, dappled light across the room.

To the right, the coffee bar stood as the heart of the café. Behind it, baristas moved with a balletic grace, their hands deftly crafting beverages with precision. A gleaming espresso machine hissed and steamed, while an array of colorful syrups and toppings were neatly aligned, ready to add their magic to any drink.

Mismatched furniture dotted the space. Some tables were of polished mahogany, others of distressed wood, and a few modern metal pieces. Velvet-cushioned chairs, leather armchairs, and cozy nooks with plush sofas added layers of texture and coziness to the setting. The flooring was a mix of polished wooden planks and ornate tiles that whispered tales of a bygone era.

At the far end of the café was a small stage, where a lone guitarist strummed a soulful tune, adding a layer of auditory serenity to the setting. Surrounding him were bookshelves, reaching almost to the ceiling, filled with classics, contemporary novels, and even a few worn-out journals, a testament to the many stories shared and created within these walls.

By one window, a terrarium garden was placed. Lush greenery, with ferns, succulents, and a small fountain, brought a touch of nature indoors. The gentle sound of trickling water melded perfectly with the soft notes of the guitar.

Taha chose a corner spot, a cozy nook with an upholstered bench seat covered in soft cushions of varying patterns. Above them, a skylight allowed the first stars of the evening to peek through.

As they settled in, a waitress, dressed in a vintage apron, approached them with a smile, setting the tone for an evening of heartfelt conversation amidst the gentle embrace of Café Luminara's charm.

As both George and taha dived once more into their conversation, George began understanding the layers of Taha's life. Beneath the tough exterior she showed the world was a vulnerable woman who had seen too much too soon. Her life was a maze of stories. She spoke about her early years, her family that struggled to make ends meet, and the decisions that pushed her into the world of night.

Taha's mother was a seamstress. Their home was always filled with the hum of the sewing machine and the colours of various fabrics. But tragedy struck early. A sudden illness took her mother away, leaving a teenage Taha with younger siblings to care for. With minimal education and no support, she made the difficult choice to enter the world's oldest profession.

However, she approached it with a strategy. Taha observed the nuances of her clients, gauging their emotions and adjusting her behaviour to offer them an experience beyond the physical. Leaning on the basic little education, she started reading books on psychology, human behaviour, and marketing. "Every human interaction is essentially an exchange," she would often say. "Be it love, business, or anything else. Understanding what the other person seeks is the key."

George was captivated by her stories, by her wisdom. He shared his own tales too—of his ascent in the world of fashion, the challenges he faced, the risks he took, and the empire he built. He talked about his passion, his dedication, and the drive that had propelled him to the top. But he also shared his vulnerabilities—the isolation, the pressure, and the overwhelming weight of success.

On another evening, they met on a beach. The beach was an expansive stretch of soft, golden sand that seemed to merge seamlessly with the horizon. As evening approached, the setting sun cast a radiant glow, painting the sky in hues of deep oranges, pinks, and purples. The line where the sky met the sea was a blur, with the sun appearing as a molten orb, ready to dip into the ocean's embrace.

The waves rolled in with a rhythmic cadence, each one crashing gently onto the shore before receding back, leaving behind a frothy lacework on the sand. The salty breeze carried whispers of distant places, ruffling the palm fronds that lined the beach's periphery and tousling George and Taha's hair.

Near the shoreline, a few children played, their laughter echoing softly, blending with the melodious chirps of the seagulls that soared overhead. Every now and then, the silhouette of a distant ship could be seen, its sails billowing, gliding gracefully over the water's shimmering surface.

Clusters of seashells, their intricate patterns, and myriad colours glistening in the fading light, lay scattered across the beach. Small tidal pools had formed in various nooks, each a miniature world of its own, teeming with tiny marine life.

Further away from the water, a few beachgoers were winding down. Some sat around makeshift bonfires, the flames dancing and casting long, flickering shadows on the sand. The soft strumming of a guitar floated in the air, accompanied by hushed voices singing along.

As George and Taha walked, they left behind a trail of footprints, momentarily etched on the sand before being claimed by the next wave. The vastness of the sea, with its infinite mysteries and depth, seemed to mirror the journey they had embarked on together—filled with discovery, challenges, and boundless possibilities.

Every so often, they would pause, allowing the waves to wash over their feet, the cool water providing a stark contrast to the warm sand beneath. They shared quiet moments, taking in the serenity of the surroundings, each lost in their thoughts yet deeply connected in that shared experience.

The beach, in all its tranquil beauty, was a space where time seemed to slow, where the weight of the world lifted, and where two souls could find solace in nature's timeless embrace.

As they laid down a yoga mat on the sand and sat on it, Taha drew parallels between her world and George's. "Both of us, in our own ways, sell dreams," she said. "You sell fashion, an image, a lifestyle. I offer solace, an escape, a fantasy. And while our worlds might seem miles apart, the essence is the same."

George pondered on this. He began to see the symmetry in their lives. They both navigated spaces where image was paramount, where understanding the audience was crucial, and where the line between reality and perception was often blurred.

These revelations made George reflect on his business strategies. He questioned the ethos of his brand, wondering if they had lost touch with the real desires of their customers. Maybe, in the race to stay ahead, they had forgotten the essence of what made them unique.

Every discussion with Taha added a new dimension to George's perspective. Their meetings, which started as an escape for him, were now sessions of enlightenment, giving him insights that no business school or consultancy could.

Yet, as they delved deeper into discussions about life and business, the boundaries of their relationship started to blur. They found comfort in each other's company, understanding in each other's stories, and a connection that went beyond words.

RETURNING TO HIS EMPIRE

The city skyscrapers pierced the early morning haze, with each building trying to assert its dominance over the horizon. But for George, the towering headquarters of his empire seemed different. It no longer appeared as the impenetrable fortress of commerce he once knew. Instead, it felt more vulnerable, mirroring his own transformed state of mind.

As his car navigated the familiar streets leading to his office, George felt a tinge of nostalgia. Every corner had a memory, every façade a story. These streets had seen him evolve from an ambitious young entrepreneur to the magnate of a global fashion empire. But the recent events, especially his serendipitous encounter with Taha, had brought him to a crossroads. His perception of success, of marketing, of human connection, had all been turned upside down.

Pulling into the underground parking, George hesitated before stepping out. The looming structure of his corporate office seemed both welcoming and foreign. Memories of board meetings, power plays, corporate politics flooded back, but so did the weight of the recent losses, the pressure to keep the brand alive, and the guilt of having possibly let down hundreds of employees who looked up to him.

The elevator ride to his floor was short but felt like an eternity. With every floor it ascended, George's heartbeat raced, the weight of his responsibilities growing heavier. His past met his present, and in those few moments, he silently deliberated if he was ready to face the future.

His secretary, Claire, greeted him with a familiar smile, but her eyes betrayed a hint of worry. "Good morning, Mr. Miller. We've missed you," she said softly, handing him a fresh cup of coffee and the day's schedule. The office was abuzz with activity, but there was an underlying tension, an unspoken concern about the company's trajectory.

George's return to the corporate headquarters was like a man reborn. The once-enthusiastic entrepreneur who had gotten lost in the quagmire of profits, losses, and business strategies now carried with him the wisdom of the streets, the wisdom of genuine human connection.

His office was a penthouse, with glass walls offering panoramic views of the city skyline. It used to be a vantage point for him, emphasizing the distance from the world below, the gap between the man at the top and the masses who adored his products. But now, it only reminded him of Taha, and her raw, emotional perspective on life. He recalled the streets she stood on, the stories she heard from her clients, the very essence of humanity that George realized had been missing from his brand.

The boardroom was filled with a palpable tension. The senior executives were well aware of the company's financial health, and the meeting's agenda was clear - a way forward. Charts were presented, graphs discussed, and marketing campaigns dissected. But amidst all the noise, George's mind kept wandering back to Taha's words, her plea for authenticity, vulnerability, and the sheer essence of human connection.

In a rare move, George stopped the meeting midway. He stood up, looked around the room, and asked a simple question. "When was the last time we touched someone's heart with our campaigns? When did we last tell a story, a genuine story?"

The room fell silent.

George began, "For too long, we have operated under the guise of marketing. But today, I want to redefine this term for our brand."

"I've had a revelation," George continued, his voice filled with newfound purpose. He proceeded to share the essence of his conversations with Taha, carefully explaining her street strategies and how they could be applied to the brand. This was obviously done without naming taha or divulging the true source of his ideas.

"I've been lost," he admitted, his voice choked with emotion. "I've been so engrossed in numbers, charts, and graphs that I lost sight of our brand's soul. But today, I've been reminded of our true essence."

"Our brand is not about clothes or fashion alone," George continued, his voice firm with newfound conviction. "It's about people, stories, dreams, and emotions. And it's high time we bring that back into our strategy."

Marketing is no longer about just selling a product; it is about telling a story, sharing an emotion, forging a genuine connection. He emphasized that it wasn't about targeting an audience but about resonating with them, understanding them, and weaving the brand into their stories.

George went on to highlight three crucial pillars for the redefined marketing strategy:

1. Authenticity: George insisted on showcasing real stories, real people. He proposed a campaign where real customers shared their experiences with the brand, their stories, their dreams, their aspirations. It was about time the brand listened and truly understood its patrons.

2. Vulnerability: Inspired by Taha's courage to be vulnerable, George suggested showing the brand's journey, challenges, struggles and all. He wanted to let the world know about the hardships, the setbacks, the moments of doubt – because it's in these imperfections that genuine connections are made.

3. Human Connection: George wanted to go back to basics. To interact with the customers, to be present, to listen. He proposed open forums, pop-up events where designers, executives, and customers could mingle, exchange ideas, and create together.

While his ideas were radical, what was even more transformative was George's passion. He spoke with an emotional fervor, with tears in his eyes, recalling Taha's wisdom, her life, and her approach to 'marketing'.

There was resistance, of course. Such a paradigm shift in thought wasn't going to be accepted without scepticism. Some executives openly scoffed at the idea, questioning the practicality of it. "With all due respect, George, are we really considering these... suggestions?" one of the executives asked incredulously.

Undeterred, George responded, "Sometimes the most profound insights come from the most unexpected sources. We've been doing things the same way for years, and where has that gotten us? It's time to think differently."

But George's conviction was infectious. The room, once filled with tension, now buzzed with excitement. Executives began sharing stories, recalling customer interactions, and realizing the immense potential of genuine, heartfelt marketing.

The meeting went on for hours, with brainstorming sessions, teams formed, and tasks assigned. By the end of it, there was a unanimous agreement - the brand was going to adopt this new marketing philosophy, one grounded in genuine human stories and emotions.

Over the next few months, George and his team worked tirelessly, creating new advertisements, events, strategies, and projects based on Taha's ideas.

The new advertisement campaign was dubbed "Real Stories, Real People." It was an ambitious project that sought to bring the authentic stories of their customers and employees to the forefront. The brand put out a call for stories, asking people to share their most memorable moments associated with the company's products. The response was overwhelming. From tales of love where couples reminisced about their first date in the brand's apparel, to stories of personal triumph where individuals wore the brand during significant milestones; the narratives were raw, real, and deeply emotional.

A team of filmmakers was roped in to document these stories. The resulting adverts were stripped of the usual glamour and glitz. There were no professional models, no staged settings. Just real people, sharing their genuine stories against the backdrop of their everyday lives. The advertisements struck a chord, resonating with viewers on a deeply emotional level. The message was clear – the brand was not just a label but an integral part of their life's journey.

With the ad campaign setting the tone, George knew that the marketing strategy had to follow suit. Traditional metrics like reach and impressions were sidelined. Instead, the focus shifted to engagement and emotional resonance. A dedicated "Listening Team" was established. Their job wasn't to sell but to listen, to understand the customers' aspirations, concerns, and feedback. This feedback loop became instrumental in shaping future product lines and campaigns.

George also initiated the "Co-creation Studios." These were spaces in select flagship stores where customers could collaborate with designers. They could share their design ideas, customize outfits, and even co-create limited edition pieces. It empowered the consumers, making them active participants in the brand's journey rather than passive recipients.

Building on the ethos of genuine human connection, George envisioned a series of events that would bridge the divide between the brand and its patrons. The first of these was "Heart-to-Heart," an open forum where company executives, designers, and customers could have candid conversations. Held in various cities, these events became a melting pot of ideas, feedback, and stories.

Next came "Fashion Unplugged." Going against the grain of traditional fashion shows, this event showcased real customers as models. They walked the ramp, not to the beats of trendy music, but narrating their personal stories associated with the brand. It was emotional, raw, and groundbreaking.

One of the most ambitious projects was the "Brand Carnival." It was a multi-day event that celebrated the brand's legacy and its patrons. Beyond shopping, it had workshops, storytelling sessions, co-creation zones, and even a dedicated space where aspiring fashionistas could pitch their ideas to the company's leadership.

Realizing that the brand had a rich history and legacy that many of the younger generation might not be familiar with, George conceived the idea of "Threads of Legacy." It was a traveling exhibition that showcased the brand's evolution through the decades.

The exhibition was meticulously curated, featuring original designs from each era, behind-the-scenes photographs of early fashion shows, and interactive displays where visitors could touch and feel fabric swatches from various periods. There were also interviews with previous designers, brand ambassadors, and even factory workers, offering a holistic view of the brand's journey.

One of the most significant attractions was a virtual reality (VR) booth where visitors could "travel" back in time to experience the brand's major milestones, from its inception to pivotal fashion shows.

To foster a deeper appreciation for the craftsmanship behind each product, George introduced "The Fabric of Dreams." These were workshops aimed at highlighting the artistry and effort that went into making each garment. Master craftsmen, tailors, and designers would offer live demonstrations of various processes – from sketching to stitching. Attendees could try their hand at designing, understanding fabric textures, and even assembling basic accessories. It was a hit among fashion students and enthusiasts, giving them a hands-on experience of the behind-the-scenes world of fashion.

George believed that fashion wasn't limited to the ramps and studios; it thrived on the streets, amidst the everyday people. To bring this vision to life, he organized "Runway Revolution" – impromptu fashion shows on city streets.

Select streets in major cities would be cordoned off for these surprise events. Local residents and shoppers would be invited to walk the ramp, showcasing their personal style. The brand's professionals would be on standby, offering quick style touch-ups and accessory add-ons, allowing participants to merge their style with the brand's offerings. These events were not just shows but celebrations of individuality and the fusion of personal style with brand aesthetics.

George's personal love for music couldn't be sidelined. "Echoes of Elegance" was a series of musical evenings held at flagship stores. Partnering with local musicians and bands, these events fused fashion with live music performances. Each event would be themed around specific eras of fashion. For instance, a jazz band would play for a 1920s themed evening, with attendees encouraged to dress in the style of that era. It was an immersive experience, letting attendees revel in the nostalgia of bygone eras while introducing them to the brand's contemporary interpretations of those styles.

Recognizing that many loyal customers had pieces from the brand's earlier years, George initiated the "Embracing the Past" bazaars. These events allowed patrons to bring in their vintage pieces, set up stalls, and sell or trade them. It was an event that celebrated the brand's heritage, giving newer fans a chance to own a piece of history. Tailors and restorers were on hand to mend and refurbish older items, ensuring they continued their journey with a new owner. Stories of each piece, from weddings to graduations, were documented and added to a digital archive, preserving the brand's intangible legacy.

George wanted to highlight the stories that garments often carry, the unseen, unspoken tales of love, loss, joy, and growth. Thus, "Whispers in the Wardrobe" was born. Inviting authors, poets, and everyday individuals, these evenings consisted of storytelling sessions where people narrated tales associated with specific pieces of clothing. Whether it was a mother's old scarf, a lover's gifted jacket, or a dress worn on a memorable date, each story added depth and emotion to the fabric, transforming them from mere garments to capsules of memories.

In a bid to involve the younger generation and get fresh perspectives, George launched the "Threads of Tomorrow." This was a design challenge targeting budding designers from fashion institutes. They were given access to the brand's archives and tasked with reimagining classic designs for the contemporary world. Winners had their designs featured in limited edition collections and received mentorship from the brand's senior designers. The event not only fostered new talent but also ensured that the brand remained innovative and relevant.

Understanding the urgent need for sustainability in the fashion industry, George introduced the "Eco Elegance" fest. This was a multi-day event promoting eco-friendly fashion practices. Workshops on upcycling, sustainable sourcing, and zero-waste fashion were the highlights. Collaborating with environmental activists and experts, the brand showcased its efforts and future plans for a more sustainable fashion journey. Attendees could also participate in crafting sessions, using scrap materials to create unique accessories, promoting the message of reuse and recycle.

George realized that while his brand had a global presence, many in the rural areas remained untouched by the world of high fashion. To bridge this gap, he organized "Fashion Frontier", where mobile fashion shows were set up in rural towns and villages. These weren't just displays but interactive events where locals were invited to merge their traditional attire with pieces from the brand, creating a beautiful fusion of global and local fashion. These events were a cultural exchange, where the brand learned as much from the rural communities as they did from the brand.

Understanding the roots of fashion means understanding the craft of weaving. George set up "Loom & Legacy" workshops in various cities where participants could come and learn the ancient art of weaving on traditional looms.

Skilled artisans were invited to teach, and participants got to take home their woven creations. This was not only an educational endeavor but also a nod to the artisans who have kept this craft alive for generations.

With a goal to highlight and support women's roles in the fashion industry, George launched the "Femme Focus" symposium. It was a day-long event featuring panel discussions, workshops, and networking opportunities for women in various roles within the industry. Topics ranged from challenges faced by women designers to the importance of promoting women-led businesses in fashion.

Recognizing the intersection of fashion and technology, George set up an expo named "Tech-Tex". Here, tech startups showcased innovations like smart fabrics, VR fitting rooms, and AI-driven fashion designs. Attendees could try out new gadgets, attend lectures on the future of fashion tech, and participate in hackathons to devise new tech solutions for the fashion industry.

George was a firm believer in celebrating global cultures. The "Global Garb" festival was a week-long extravaganza that spotlighted fashion from different corners of the world. Each day was dedicated to a specific continent, featuring runway shows, food stalls, music, and dance from that region. It was a melting pot of cultures, and attendees could take a fashion journey around the world without leaving the venue.

Transparency in fashion manufacturing was becoming increasingly important for conscious consumers. To address this, George organized "Behind the Seams" events, where loyal customers and enthusiasts could sign up for factory tours. They got a firsthand view of how their favorite garments were produced, the safety measures in place, and the sustainability practices adopted. Post-tour, senior members from the brand held Q&A sessions, addressing any concerns and queries.

Merging the worlds of art and fashion, George initiated a unique event where contemporary artists were given a white dress or suit as a canvas. The "Artistic Attire" event culminated in an exhibition where these transformed garments were displayed as art pieces. Attendees could bid on these unique pieces, with proceeds going to charity.

Each event was a testament to George's transformed vision for the brand. It was no longer just about commerce; it was about community, connection, and a shared love for fashion that told stories.

Every event was meticulously planned and executed, reflecting George's unwavering commitment to reinvigorating the brand's presence in the fashion world while ensuring it remained rooted in values of education, transparency, and global appreciation. These events were not just about clothes but about living and experiencing stories, memories, and connections.

George often attended these events, not as the MD of a multi-billion dollar company but as a humble listener. He laughed, cried, and celebrated with the attendees, forging genuine connections.

The sales figures began to reflect this change. Profits soared, not because of aggressive marketing tactics, but because the brand had touched people's hearts. It became a movement, a revolution that changed not just the company's fortunes but also the entire fashion industry's approach.

But for George, it was more personal. Every time he saw a happy customer, every time he heard a genuine story, he was reminded of Taha, the woman from the streets, the brilliant marketer, the genius psychologist. She had changed his life, his perspective, and in doing so, had redefined marketing for an entire generation.

The empire that once seemed on the verge of collapse was now rising like a phoenix, all because of a simple yet profound realization – at its core, every business is about human connections. And George, with Taha's wisdom and the unwavering support of his team, was determined to make that the cornerstone of his renewed empire.

George's efforts were not without challenges. There was initial skepticism, both internally and externally. Many believed that this emotional, story-driven approach would be a passing fad. But as months turned into years, the brand's transformation was undeniable. Customers felt a deep-seated loyalty, not just because of the products but due to the genuine human connections they experienced. Sales soared, but more importantly, the brand narrative shifted from mere fashion to stories, dreams, and genuine human connection.

As the sun set on another day, George stood by his office window, looking down at the bustling streets, a world he was now deeply connected to. And in the distance, he could almost hear the hauntingly beautiful notes of a song of love, connection, and genuine human stories.

෯෴

BATTLING SCEPTICISM

The revival of George's empire wasn't just a story of resurgence; it was also a tale of confronting scepticism. Every profound change is met with resistance, and George's new vision for his company, inspired by Taha's unconventional insights, was no different.

The marketing department, once the crown jewel of his organization, had grown complacent. Used to their tried and tested formulas, they believed they knew best. The ideas George now brought to the table, ideas he credited to an "external consultant" to protect Taha's identity, were seen as too radical, too distant from the world of haute couture.

Sarah Collins, the Vice President of Marketing, was the first to voice her reservations. An Ivy League graduate with impeccable credentials, she had been with the company for a decade. "George," she began in a team meeting, choosing her words carefully, "while I respect the need for change, I believe we should proceed with caution. Our brand has a legacy, an image. We cannot simply flip the script based on one person's perspective."

The room grew tense. Everyone knew how much George valued Sarah's opinions. They had collaborated on countless successful campaigns in the past. But George's recent revelations had changed him, and there was a newfound firmness in his eyes.

"I understand your concerns, Sarah," George responded, his voice steady. "But sometimes, an outsider's perspective can shed light on things we've been blind to. Our brand's legacy isn't just in the clothes we sell but the stories we tell, the lives we touch. We need a shift, a genuine one."

Sarah wasn't alone in her scepticism. Whispers filled the hallways. Questions were raised. "Is George losing his touch?" "Why is he betting the future of our company on such untested ideas?" "Who is this mysterious consultant guiding our fate?"

The sceptics came in full force with all guns blazing, they raised the following objections:

Dilution of Brand Image: A major concern voiced by many, especially industry experts, was that George's strategy would dilute the brand's luxurious image. "High fashion is aspirational," remarked François Devereux, a respected voice in the fashion journalism community, in a widely circulated op-ed. "By aligning with street styles and embracing the tales of the everyday, there's a risk of the brand becoming pedestrian, losing its allure."

Financial Risk: Many financial analysts believed that the brand was taking an unnecessary risk. "Investing in a completely new direction when the current one isn't broken is financial hara-kiri," commented Stella Ferreira from the finance magazine 'Market Maven'.

Disconnect with Target Audience: Critics believed that the core audience, which was used to exclusivity, wouldn't relate to the 'common' stories. Jessica Lin, an influencer with a massive following, voiced her reservations: "I love the brand because it sets me apart. But if it starts looking like something picked from a street stall, why would I pay a premium?"

Too Much, Too Soon: Some insiders felt that while change was necessary, the pace at which George was introducing these transformations was too rapid. "It's like trying to turn a cruise ship on a dime," mused Aaron Holt, a senior designer in the company.

Authenticity or Gimmick?: This was perhaps the most biting criticism. Some believed that George's attempt to integrate street style and personal stories was just a marketing gimmick, a passing phase that lacked genuine authenticity. Melissa Graft, a fashion blogger, wrote: "Today it's street stories, tomorrow it could be space fashion. It's all about what's trending, not what's genuine."

George was no stranger to criticism. Yet, the sheer volume and intensity of scepticism took him aback. But with his vision clear and Taha's wisdom ringing in his ears, he decided to address each concern systematically.

Defending the Brand's Evolution: In response to the fear of dilution of the brand's image, George held a press conference. "Luxury isn't merely about price tags or exclusivity," he began. "True luxury lies in experiences, in stories, in the craftsmanship. By incorporating street styles, we're not lowering our standards. Instead, we're elevating those unseen, unsung artisans to the pedestal they deserve."

The Financial Perspective: Addressing the financial concerns, George presented data. He highlighted burgeoning global trends where consumers increasingly sought brands with depth, authenticity, and a social conscience. "Our shift isn't just ideological; it's strategic. The consumer today wants more than just a product; they want a narrative, a soul, a connection. Our new direction aligns with this global shift."

Connecting with a Broader Audience: To the fears of alienating the existing audience, George had a candid reply. "Fashion is universal. While we value our core audience and will continue to cater to them, we also see a vast, untapped market that resonates with real stories. Our aim is to strike a balance, ensuring that while we bring in fresh perspectives, our loyalists still see the brand they love."

Pace of Change: George agreed with the concerns about the rapid transformations but defended his stance passionately. "Sometimes, to break free from inertia, a jolt is necessary. While the pace of external changes may seem rapid, these are ideas and strategies we've been mulling over for a long time."

Genuine Authenticity: The criticism about authenticity stung, but George faced it head-on. He organized workshops where employees, critics, and the media could meet the artisans, hear their stories, and witness the craftsmanship. "This isn't a passing phase," he declared. "This is a heartfelt homage to craftsmanship and stories. Our collaboration with street artisans isn't a marketing gimmick; it's a bridge, connecting worlds, celebrating fashion in its purest form."

George's responses weren't just verbal rebuttals. They were actions, campaigns, initiatives, and events that showcased his commitment to the new vision. With each step, he wasn't merely defending his stance but was educating, enlightening, and drawing everyone into the brand's new world.

The media caught wind of the changes afoot. Critics had a field day, predicting the company's downfall, attributing it to George's midlife crisis or even speculating about a secret love affair influencing his decisions. The world outside was cynical, but what hurt George more was the doubt within his own walls.

Each day posed a new challenge. Decisions were second-guessed, campaigns debated, and every step forward was met with two steps back. But amidst this storm of skepticism, Taha's words became George's anchor. Every evening, he'd find solace in their deep conversations, drawing strength from her wisdom.

One evening, as George shared his frustrations, Taha mused, "You know, in my line of work, scepticism is a constant companion. Every client, every passerby, every judgmental gaze is a question, a doubt. But I've learned that if you believe in your worth, in the authenticity of your offering, scepticism can't touch you."

Emboldened by her words, George decided to face the scepticism head-on. He organized a company-wide town hall meeting. The massive auditorium was packed with employees, every eye fixed on the stage, awaiting George's address.

Taking a deep breath, George began, "I know many of you are sceptical of the direction we're taking. I understand your fears and apprehensions. But I ask you to trust the journey. Trust the heart and soul we're infusing into our brand. Our legacy isn't set in stone; it's alive, evolving, and we have the chance to shape it."

He began by acknowledging the elephant in the room – the brand's declining sales and market position. He spoke about the need for change, for innovative strategies, and most importantly, for the courage to look beyond conventional wisdom.

Then, sharing Taha's insights, George passionately pitched each strategy, emphasizing the core philosophy behind them. He spoke of personalization, storytelling, creating authentic connections, anticipating needs, embracing imperfections, and continuous innovation.

The impact was palpable. The auditorium echoed with applause, eyes glistened with tears, and a newfound energy surged through the crowd. The scepticism hadn't vanished, but it had been met with a powerful counterforce – emotion.

Over the subsequent weeks, George's leadership took on a collaborative tone. He held brainstorming sessions with different departments, inviting fresh perspectives, encouraging debates, and fostering a culture of shared ownership. Slowly but surely, the walls of scepticism began to crumble.

Sarah, once George's fiercest critic, started seeing the potential in his vision. In an emotional conversation, she admitted, "George, I was afraid. Afraid of losing the brand

I loved, the legacy we built. But now I see that we're not losing it; we're enriching it."

As months rolled by, the company's campaigns began to reflect its renewed ethos. Stories took centre stage, authenticity shone through, and the world began to take notice. The critics, once scathing in their reviews, were now penning praises, admiring the brand's audacity to redefine itself.

But George knew the battle wasn't over. Scepticism, like old habits, dies hard. Yet, with Taha's wisdom in his heart and a team united in purpose, he was ready to face whatever came next, turning doubters into believers, one story at a time.

A RESURGENCE OF HOPE

The headquarters of George Miller's empire was a beacon of grandeur. Tall, impressive, and bearing the insignia of a brand recognized worldwide. But a few months ago, the building felt more like a mausoleum than a hive of activity. Sales had slumped, creativity had stagnated, and the hallways echoed with whispered concerns rather than buoyant laughter.

However, winds of change were sweeping through, driven by George's renewed passion and Taha's invaluable insights. As the duo's unconventional strategies began to yield results, a newfound hope began to permeate the company.

One morning, as George walked through the headquarters, he noticed something he hadn't seen in a long while. The design team, usually buried in sketches, was laughing and animatedly discussing something. Intrigued, George approached and found them engrossed in a montage of old campaigns, comparing them with newer ideas.

"Look at this," exclaimed Lisa, a young designer pointing at a vintage ad. "I mean, it's classic, yes, but it's so...

predictable. With our new direction, there's a pulse, a heartbeat. It's alive!"

George smiled, watching his team rekindle their love for their craft. The seed of hope was sprouting.

The resurgence wasn't limited to the design department. The sales team, who once dreaded meetings due to declining numbers, now had an enthusiasm that was palpable. The boardroom, which had previously been a place of tension, transformed into a hub of dynamic discussions and innovative ideas.

Karen, a long-time sales manager, shared at one such meeting, "I visited our flagship store yesterday. The energy is different. Customers aren't just shopping; they're engaging. They want to know the stories behind our designs, the ethos of our brand. It's like they've rediscovered us."

It wasn't just the internal teams that felt the change; the world outside was taking notice. Fashion magazines, once critical of the brand's stagnation, now featured extensive editorials praising its daring revival. Social media was abuzz with influencers and fans lauding the brand's new campaigns, which resonated on a deeply emotional level.

At a high-profile fashion event, George was taken aback when a renowned fashion critic, known for her sharp words, approached him. "George," she began, her stern face softening into a rare smile, "I've watched brands rise and fall, but what you've done with yours, the rebirth, it's... exceptional. It's like watching a phoenix rise. Bravo."

The affirmation was gratifying. But for George, it wasn't just about reclaiming the brand's place in the spotlight. It was about restoring hope to every individual associated with his empire. Every employee, from the janitor to top-tier managers, needed to believe in the brand's magic again.

George started organizing monthly "Hope Gatherings" - events where teams across departments would come together, share stories, celebrate successes, and discuss challenges. These weren't just corporate meetings; they were soulful reunions. The atmosphere was electric, filled with stories of personal triumphs, tales of obstacles overcome, and dreams for the future.

One particularly memorable gathering saw Maria, a veteran seamstress, take the stage. Her voice quivered with emotion as she shared, "I've been with this company for 25 years. I've stitched countless designs, poured my soul into every thread. When we began to falter, it felt like my life's work was unraveling. But now, seeing our creations worn with pride, knowing they carry stories and emotions, it's like my purpose has been renewed."

Tears filled George's eyes as he listened. This was the hope he had yearned for.

Yet, it wasn't all smooth sailing. As the brand gained momentum, challenges arose. Counterfeit products flooded the market, competitors launched smear campaigns, and supply chain issues threatened production. But the company faced these challenges differently now. Instead of panic, there was determination. Instead of blame, there was collaboration. Hope, it seemed, wasn't just a fleeting emotion; it was a powerful force driving them forward.

One evening, as George sat in his expansive office, overlooking the city's twinkling skyline, Taha called. "I saw your latest campaign," she said, her voice filled with pride. "I loved it and so did many people I know."

George chuckled, "Yes, it is. Thank you Taha. All this could not have happened without you."

As they talked, George realized that his business wasn't just about selling clothes and building a brand but rather it was about touching lives. In Taha, he had found not just a saviour for his empire but a beacon of hope for his soul.

The resurgence of his brand was a testament to the human spirit's resilience. When fuelled by genuine emotion, guided by authentic intent, and anchored in hope, even the most colossal empires could rise from the ashes. The journey had just begun, but with hope as their compass, the horizon seemed brighter than ever.

TAHA'S SECOND LESSON

The glow of revitalized success hung around the empire like an aura. George's brand was making headlines, and the credit largely went to Taha's wisdom. George had always believed in lifelong learning, but little did he know that his most profound lessons would come from a woman society had marginalized.

Taha's first lesson had drastically shifted the company's marketing approach. Her unique insights on customer relationships and understanding had worked wonders. Still, as George knew, resting on one's laurels was a dangerous game. He called Taha for further meetings, eager to glean more of her wisdom. However, there was a difference. This time he called taha to his house.

The sun had set, casting a golden hue over the city. George's upscale apartment, with its panoramic windows, was the perfect backdrop for a session of brainstorming and idea generation. As Taha stepped in, the stark contrast between their worlds became evident. Yet, in that room, societal constructs melted away, leaving two brilliant minds, eager to collaborate.

"Thank you for coming, Taha," George began, pouring wine for them both. "Our last few meetings have changed everything. But I can't help but feel there's more we can do. More we can learn from your unique experience."

Taha sipped her wine, her gaze distant, reflecting on her tumultuous journey. "You know, George," she began softly, "The world of my profession is layered. Tonight, I want to talk about trust."

George leaned forward, intrigued. "Go on."

"In my world, every interaction is built on a delicate balance of trust," she started. "A customer trusts me with their vulnerabilities, their secrets. In return, I trust them with my safety, my well-being. It's a silent pact. Trust isn't just about being reliable; it's about creating a space where the other person feels seen, valued, and understood."

She paused, letting the weight of her words sink in. "Your brand isn't just selling clothes, George. You're selling an experience, a promise. Your customers need to trust that promise."

George nodded slowly. "But how do we build that trust, especially after our recent setbacks?"

Taha smiled. "By showing genuine care. Every interaction, whether it's a customer walking into your store or someone browsing your online site, needs to feel personalized and genuine. Listen to their stories, their needs. Tailor their experience, not just based on what they buy, but on who they are."

She continued, "In my line of work, I've had clients who didn't always want what they initially came for. Some just needed someone to talk to, to feel connected. I had to read between the lines, understand the unsaid."

Taha's eyes glistened with unshed tears. "One evening, a young man, probably in his early twenties, approached me. His eyes, George, they were filled with pain. As we talked, I realized he wasn't there for physical intimacy. He was grieving the loss of his girlfriend. He just needed a human connection, someone to hold, to share his pain with. That night, I was his confidante, his shoulder to cry on."

She took a deep breath. "That's the depth of trust we need to build with our customers. Understand them beyond their wallets. What are their dreams, their fears, their desires?"

George was visibly moved. "That's...profound, Taha. But how do we translate that into our business?"

"Engage with them," she replied. "Hold events where they can share their fashion stories. How did they feel wearing your brand on their first date, their job interview, their graduation? Create platforms where they can voice their opinions on your designs, suggest improvements. Make them feel part of your brand's journey."

Taha's passion was infectious. "Empower your sales staff. Train them not just to sell but to connect, to empathize. Use technology, not as a mere selling tool, but as a bridge to understand your customer's preferences and tailor their shopping experience."

She paused; her gaze intense. "But most importantly, be authentic. People can sense pretence. If you genuinely care, they'll trust you. And trust, George, is the most potent currency."

The room was silent, the weight of Taha's words pressing down. George felt like he was in the presence of a sage, her wisdom born from experiences most couldn't fathom.

"I...I'm overwhelmed, Taha," George confessed. "Your insights, they're revolutionary. We've been so focused on profits that we've forgotten the human aspect."

Taha reached out, her hand covering his. "That's the world, George. In our race for more, we often forget the core - human connection. But it's never too late to change. Start small, be consistent, and the trust will build."

As the evening wore on, George and Taha delved deeper, charting out strategies and plans. By the time the first light of dawn painted the sky, they had laid the foundation for a new era for George's empire. An era rooted in trust, understanding, and genuine care.

As Taha left, George felt a mix of gratitude and admiration. Her lessons, derived from her challenging life, were invaluable. Little did society know that behind the label of a 'prostitute' was a woman with the wisdom to transform empires. And George was ready to let the world see that.

ঙ৵৹

THE OFFER

As the brand's revival took root, George found himself increasingly reliant on Taha's insights. Their collaboration had proved more beneficial than he could have ever imagined. But the true weight of their association went beyond numbers or profit margins; it lay in the realization that Taha's life experiences and wisdom were invaluable assets to the business world.

One evening, as they sat in a quiet corner of a café, George broached a subject he had been contemplating for weeks. "Taha," he began, hesitating slightly, "Have you ever considered leaving the streets?. I want to introduce you to the world. I want you to be part of my company. What if I offered you a position in the company?"

Taha looked taken aback. Her life had always revolved around the streets, its rules, its survival tactics. The idea of transitioning to a corporate world, with its own challenges and nuances, was daunting. But George's offer was genuine, his eyes reflecting the earnestness of his proposal.

"It's not out of pity, Taha," George clarified, sensing her apprehension. "It's because I truly believe that your perspective, your understanding of human behavior and needs, is something our brand desperately needs. You've already proved it."

After days of introspection, Taha decided to accept the offer.

George's office, boasted a panoramic view of the city's expanse. Each morning, as he looked out, he was reminded of his empire's enormity and the responsibility that came with it.

But today was different.

The room was a whirl of activity. Reporters from leading fashion magazines, influencers with millions of followers, and industry experts all waited in anticipation. George was about to unveil a new marketing strategy, one that would change the trajectory of his company. But more than the strategy, it was the mastermind behind it that had everyone curious. Rumors had spread like wildfire, speculating on this mysterious advisor who had transformed the floundering empire.

As the clock struck 10, George stepped onto the stage, his confidence evident. "Ladies and gentlemen," he began, "Thank you for being here today. I stand before you, not as the savior of my brand, but as a humble student who had the privilege of learning from an incredible teacher."

The room was silent, hanging on to every word.

"Many of you have been speculating about the genius behind our company's resurgence. Today, I am proud to introduce her to you." George gestured to the side, and Taha walked forward, her poise and grace evident.

There was an audible gasp. Whispers filled the room. "A prostitute?" "Is this some kind of joke?" "Has George lost his mind?" The prejudice and skepticism were palpable.

George, sensing the room's mood, continued, "I understand your surprise. Our society often blinds us with labels, obscuring the immense talent and wisdom that lie beneath. Taha, despite her profession, has an understanding of human nature, customer relationship, and genuine trust that even the best business schools cannot teach."

Taha, standing tall, began her address. Her voice, though soft, carried a weight and conviction. "My life's journey has been... unconventional," she began, choosing her words carefully. "Every night, I navigated the intricate maze of human emotions and desires. My livelihood depended on understanding my clients, creating a bond of trust, and ensuring their satisfaction."

The room was rapt. Taha's eloquence, combined with her raw honesty, was mesmerizing. "Each one of us is selling something," she continued, "Whether it's a product, a service, or ourselves. The key lies in understanding and connecting with those we serve."

She went on to share insights from her life, drawing parallels between her experiences and modern marketing principles. The audience was taken on an emotional journey, from the streets' dark alleys to the high-powered boardrooms, showing them that wisdom could be found in the most unexpected places.

"When George first approached me, it wasn't my services he sought. He was burdened with the weight of a failing empire. Our conversations, however, uncovered profound marketing truths." Taha elaborated on the strategies they had devised, explaining the importance of trust, genuine care, and understanding in creating lasting customer relationships.

The room was a mix of emotions. Some were moved to tears, resonating with Taha's powerful narrative. Others were still skeptical, unable to look past her profession. Yet, no one could deny the transformation she had brought about in George's brand.

As the presentation concluded, the floor was opened for questions. One reporter, a young woman with a determined glint in her eye, asked, "Taha, how do you handle the prejudice and judgment, especially in a world that's quick to label?"

Taha smiled gently, "By knowing my worth. By understanding that my experiences, no matter how unconventional, have value. And by believing that every individual has the potential for brilliance, regardless of societal labels."

The day was filled with interviews, discussions, and strategy breakdowns. Taha, with George by her side, navigated each interaction with grace and poise, winning over many skeptics. As the sun began its descent, painting the sky with hues of orange and pink, George and Taha stood by the window, reflecting on the day.

"You were incredible," George murmured, admiration evident in his eyes.

Taha smiled, "It was our combined brilliance, George. Today was just the beginning."

As night enveloped the city, two souls, worlds apart yet united by a shared vision, stood together. The empire was not only on the path to recovery but was also setting new standards, redefining marketing, and challenging societal prejudices.

Unveiling brilliance, it turned out, was not just about revealing a strategy. It was about highlighting the latent potential that resides in every individual, waiting for the right moment, the right opportunity, to shine.

൭൦ൢ

From the Streets to the Boardroom

Taha's journey from the labyrinthine streets to the opulent boardrooms wasn't a mere switch of physical locations. It was, in essence, a transcendence through socio-economic layers, prejudices, and personal evolutions. As much as it was about her unyielding spirit, it was equally about the society's readiness (or lack thereof) to accept her.

For someone rooted deeply in the raw realities of the streets, the initial foray into corporate life was nothing short of bewildering. The towering skyscrapers, the swift elevators zipping through floors, and the silent, often judgmental, corridors were all alien to her. The meetings, with their structured formalities, felt like orchestrated plays where everyone knew their lines except her.

But Taha's strength was her keen observational skills. She had survived the streets by reading people, by discerning intentions hidden behind smiles or threats. She applied this same acumen in decoding the nuances of corporate politics and dynamics.

The initial days were challenging. The corporate world, with its suits, ties, and formal lexicons, was a stark contrast to the raw streets she was familiar with. Taha often found herself drowning amidst terminologies she barely understood. The rigid protocols and etiquette seemed like an elaborate dance, a choreography she was yet to master.

Yet, her essence remained unchanged. She may have traded her provocative attire for elegant business suits, but her instinct, the very core that made her so astutely understanding of people, remained untamed and fierce. In the first few weeks, she observed, absorbing the dynamics of this new world like a sponge.

The transition, however, was far from seamless. Walking into the company's headquarters on her first day, Taha felt like a fish out of water. The polished floors, the chic décor, the organized chaos—it was worlds apart from the alleys she had known.

But what proved most challenging was the reception she received. While some employees were curious and welcoming, others were openly skeptical, even resentful. Whispers echoed through the corridors. "From the streets to the boardroom? What could she possibly bring to the table?"

Taha, however, was no stranger to adversity. She began her tenure not by imposing her ideas but by patiently observing, understanding the corporate culture, its dynamics, and its challenges.

George's office was a sprawling expanse of luxury. Overlooking the city's skyline, it bore witness to many strategic discussions, heated debates, and momentous decisions. It was in this very office that Taha had her first corporate meeting.

The long mahogany table gleamed under the chandeliers. Seated around it were top executives of the empire, their sharp gazes occasionally drifting towards Taha. The air was thick with scepticism. She could feel it — the silent questions, the doubtful glances. For many in the room, her place at that table was a far-fetched reality they were struggling to accept.

The meeting began with George outlining the challenges the company was facing. As numbers were discussed and graphs projected, Taha listened intently. While the jargon was foreign, the underlying emotions — the fear, the desperation, the hope — were all too familiar to her.

When George finally turned to her, inviting her to share her perspective, the room went silent. The atmosphere in the opulent boardroom was palpable. The hush of anticipation, the discreet shuffling of documents, and the murmured exchanges. At the head of the long mahogany table stood Taha, the embodiment of raw experience meeting structured corporatism.

She began, her voice clear and strong, "In both our worlds, the streets and the corporate empire, the essence of success boils down to one crucial factor: connection."

"Out on the streets," Taha began, "it's not just about the allure or the physical appeal. It's about building a bridge of trust in a matter of minutes. The same goes for business. Your customers might be drawn by an advertisement or a discount, but they'll stay loyal only if they trust your brand."

She emphasized, "When a client approached me, their trust was hard-won. They needed assurance, not just of the services but of discretion, safety, and understanding. Similarly, your customers need to trust that your product delivers on its promise, that their data is safe with you, and that you value their loyalty."

"In my world, understanding the unsaid is a skill honed out of necessity. Not every client verbalized their needs, some were masked behind layers of societal pressure, personal fears, or insecurities. Deciphering that was crucial." Taha's gaze swept the room. "In business, isn't it the same? Aren't customers often unable to articulate exactly what they seek?

It's up to us to read between the lines, anticipate their needs, and over-deliver." "I had to be acutely attuned to the unsaid. A hesitation in their voice, a fleeting look of uncertainty, these were cues, indicating their unspoken needs or concerns." Taha elaborated, "In the business sector, these nuances translate to customer reviews, feedback forms, and purchasing patterns. Are you listening closely enough?"

"The streets taught me to be fluid, to adapt based on the client, the location, and the situation. Each night was a lesson in recalibrating strategies. In the business realm, the market is equally unpredictable. Trends shift, economies fluctuate, and customer preferences evolve. A brand's survival depends on its ability to adapt swiftly and efficiently."

"The world I come from is unpredictable. Every night presented a different set of challenges. Adaptability was not a choice; it was a necessity." Her gaze swept across the room, "The business environment, too, is volatile. Changing market dynamics, technological disruptions, geopolitical shifts – they all demand agility and adaptability from brands."

"On the streets, the initial draw might be an evocative gaze or an enticing attire, much like an advertisement or a compelling marketing campaign in your world. These serve as gateways, introductions to a promise of something more. But remember, they are merely door openers. What truly matters is what lies beyond."

"A generic approach never worked for me. Each client was unique, with distinct needs and expectations. Offering a tailored experience was the differentiator." Taha continued, "Isn't it the same for your customers? Don't they seek products or services that feel made for them? Brands need to stop looking at customers as demographics and start viewing them as individuals."

"No two nights were the same for me. Each client was an individual, seeking a unique experience, tailored to their desires. Customization wasn't just a strategy; it was a lifeline." Taha's voice held passion, "In your realm, personalizing a customer's experience, making them feel seen and valued, is the key to ensuring their loyalty."

Taha took a deep breath, emphasizing her next point, "But, perhaps the most significant parallel is authenticity. Pretence was easily seen through in my world. The streets demanded raw, unfiltered authenticity. So does your customer. In a world inundated with marketing gimmicks, authentic brand stories and genuine customer engagements stand out."

"But, while there are parallels, there are stark differences too. For me, a misjudgement could mean a life-threatening situation. The stakes were incredibly high, every single time." Taha's voice grew softer, more introspective. "Here, in the corporate world, you have safety nets – market research, advisory boards, contingency plans. You have the luxury to fail, learn, and rebuild."

Drawing her speech to a close, Taha's eyes shimmered with conviction, "Despite the differences, the core remains unchanged. It's about understanding humans, building trust, and delivering value. Whether on the gritty streets or in this plush boardroom, genuine human connection is the cornerstone of success."

The room remained silent long after she had finished. It was as if they were processing, trying to reconcile the world she came from with the truths she presented. It was the CFO, a stern middle-aged man, who broke the silence. "While your experiences are... unique," he said hesitantly, "they bring a fresh perspective, something we've been lacking."

As days turned into weeks, Taha became more entrenched in the operations of the empire. She attended meetings, collaborated on strategies, and even spearheaded a few initiatives. Her unconventional wisdom was now sought after, with departments vying for her insights.

Her transformation was not just limited to her professional growth. The employees, who had once looked at her with disdain, now greeted her with respect. Her evenings, once spent in the loneliness of her apartment, were now filled with invitations to dinners and events. The world was finally seeing Taha, the woman of substance, and not just the label society had thrust upon her.

However, the journey was not devoid of challenges. There were days when her past haunted her, when the whispers and rumors became too loud to ignore. But with George by her side, supporting and guiding her, Taha faced each challenge head-on.

One evening, as they sat in George's office, he turned to her, "You've changed the fate of this empire, Taha. But more importantly, you've changed the narrative. From the streets to this boardroom, you've proven that brilliance is not bound by circumstances."

Taha smiled, "It's not about where we come from, George. It's about where we're headed. I had a teacher in you, someone who saw beyond the prejudice. This boardroom? It's just a testament to what can be achieved when we're given a chance."

As night enveloped the city, the lights from the skyscrapers shimmered like a million stars. And in that vast expanse, in an office high above, two souls celebrated a journey — one of resilience, determination, and breaking barriers. From the streets to the boardroom, Taha's journey was a beacon of hope, proving that with the right opportunities and belief, anyone could redefine their destiny.

၈ဝ၀

EMBRACING CHANGE

Change is a constant, they say. Yet for most people, it remains an intimidating force, something to be wary of or even avoid. It entails letting go of the familiar, the comfort zones we've built over the years. But sometimes, it's change that becomes the catalyst for true growth, for rediscovering one's purpose, and for building relationships that last a lifetime.

George Miller's life, though it seemed set in its grandeur, was facing a season of change. The empire he had constructed was wobbling, and the ground beneath seemed unsteady. But more than the potential financial losses, it was the idea of his legacy crumbling that haunted him.

Taha, on the other hand, had seen countless seasons of change. From the numerous alleys she had walked through, the countless faces she had encountered, to the many storms she had weathered—change was a close companion. Yet, every new dawn brought with it a renewed sense of purpose, a determination to face another day, to adapt, to survive.

As the two sat in George's plush office, surrounded by charts and figures reflecting future plans and strategies for growth, the air was thick with tension. His team, all adorned in sharp suits, presented strategy after strategy, hoping to find a solution, a way out of the maze.

But Taha saw something they didn't. It wasn't just about numbers or sales strategies. It was about evolving, about understanding the pulse of the market, about listening to the heartbeat of their consumers.

She remembered a rainy evening from her past. The streets were slick with water, and she had taken shelter under a tattered awning. Next to her was an old woman selling handmade trinkets. Business was slow, and the woman seemed lost in thought. As Taha struck a conversation, the woman shared her story. She spoke of how she had once been the toast of the town, with her handcrafted jewelry being sought after. But as times changed and machine-made goods flooded the market, her craft lost its charm. She had resisted change, holding on to traditions, until she found herself on the streets, her glory days long gone.

"That's the thing about change," the old woman had whispered, her eyes distant. "You can either embrace it and evolve, or resist and get left behind."

Those words echoed in Taha's mind as she addressed George's team. "We need to adapt," she began, her voice steady. "We need to understand that our consumers are evolving. Their desires, their preferences are changing. We cannot offer them yesterday's designs and expect them to buy. We need to understand their stories, their aspirations, and reflect that in our collections."

There was a hushed silence in the room. This was a perspective they hadn't considered. The conversation shifted from mere numbers to understanding consumer psychology, to embracing the winds of change and charting a new course.

George, inspired by Taha's words, organized focus groups, inviting loyal customers and new prospects, aiming to listen, to truly understand. Taha, with her innate ability to connect with people, led these sessions, drawing out stories, aspirations, and dreams.

What emerged was a tapestry of desires. A young woman wanted eco-friendly fabrics, a reflection of her commitment to the environment. A middle-aged man sought designs that combined tradition with modernity, echoing his journey of balancing his roots with the demands of a globalized world. A teenager desired bold, edgy designs, a testament to her rebellious phase.

As the company began to incorporate these insights, change became palpable. The design studios buzzed with creativity, as designers drew inspiration from real stories, creating collections that resonated, that told tales.

But the change wasn't just external. George, once resistant to altering his tried and tested methods, began to see the beauty of evolution. He realized that to sustain, one had to adapt, to keep pace with the ever-shifting sands of time.

Taha, too, witnessed a transformation. From the alleys to the boardroom, her journey was a testament to the power of resilience, of embracing one's past while charting a new future. Her influence was evident, not just in the company's strategy but in the very ethos. She became the beacon of change, inspiring teams to think differently, to be unafraid of charting unknown territories.

As months turned into years, the company not only regained its lost glory but soared to new heights. Their collections, a blend of tradition and modernity, of sustainability and style, became the talk of the town. They weren't just selling clothes; they were selling dreams, aspirations, stories.

Honestly, it wasn't just about embracing change; it was about understanding its essence. It was about realizing that change wasn't an external force but an internal evolution. It was about understanding that the only way to truly grow was to let go of the familiar and step into the unknown, hand in hand with change.

For George and Taha, their journey together became a testament to the beauty of transformation, of finding strength in vulnerability, of rediscovering purpose amidst chaos. Embracing change wasn't just a strategy; it was a way of life, a dance with the inevitable, a celebration of the new while honouring the old.

A UNION OF MINDS

Taha had made her mark in the corporate realm, no longer seen as a mere outsider but as a force that drove change. Her uncanny ability to read people, to understand their unspoken needs, was the result of her years on the streets. The very skills that had once been her tools of survival were now reshaping the empire. But beyond the corporate strategies and sales upticks, there was a deeper connection brewing — one that transcended business charts and models. It was the union of two brilliant minds.

George's penthouse, high above the city, had become their haven. Their meetings, initially strictly professional, had evolved into intense brainstorming sessions, where ideas flowed freely. The penthouse, with its expansive glass walls, seemed to encapsulate the world, yet protected them from its judgments.

One evening, as the city's skyline bathed in the golden hue of sunset, George spread out an array of design sketches on the table. They were potential designs for the next fashion line. "Taha," he began, his eyes scanning the illustrations, "these designs were created by the best in the business.

But I need you to look at them, to tell me if they evoke any emotions, any stories."

Taha leaned forward, her fingers tracing the lines and patterns. For her, these weren't just designs; they were narratives waiting to be told. She paused at one particular sketch. It depicted a woman, fierce yet vulnerable, draped in fabrics that seemed to dance around her. "This," she whispered, "reminds me of my life. The strength, the struggle, the hope... It's all here."

George watched her, captivated. He saw the passion in her eyes, the raw emotion that welled up as she connected with the design. "That's it, Taha! Fashion isn't just about clothes; it's about stories. We need to narrate tales that resonate, that tug at heartstrings."

Their discussions stretched into the night, weaving tales from threads, creating stories that the world would wear. Every design, every color, and every pattern became a character in their shared narrative.

It was during these sessions that their intellectual connection deepened. They began to see the world through each other's eyes. Taha introduced George to the labyrinth of streets she knew so well, showing him the pulse of the city, the raw, unfiltered realities that were often overlooked. George, in turn, opened the world of fashion to Taha, revealing the intricacies of design and the artistry behind every creation.

Their worlds, so starkly different, began to merge, creating a fusion rich in experiences and insights. They discussed everything, from the socio-economic factors influencing fashion trends to the deep-seated human desires that drive consumption.

One evening, as they sat surrounded by fabric samples and design sketches, Taha hesitated, then began, "George, there's something I've been meaning to share. A story from my past, something that might give us a fresh perspective."

She spoke of a night years ago, a particularly cold winter evening when she had met a young woman on the streets. The woman, barely in her twenties, was new to the city and had nowhere to go. Taha had shared her makeshift shelter, and they had huddled together for warmth. As the night wore on, the young woman had pulled out a small, tattered sketchbook, revealing exquisite designs, dreams captured on paper. She had been a budding fashion designer, forced onto the streets by circumstances. But even in her despair, she clung to her dreams, her sketches a testament to her undying passion.

Taha's voice wavered as she continued, "That woman didn't survive the winter. But her dreams, her sketches, they stayed with me. I believe we can bring them to life, honor her memory."

George, deeply moved, took Taha's hand. "We will. Together, we will weave her dreams into our narrative."

Their bond, already strong, solidified further. They weren't just business associates; they were collaborators in the truest sense, their minds meeting at an intersection of creativity and experience.

As weeks morphed into months, the new fashion line began to take shape. The designs, deeply rooted in real stories, resonated with the masses. People weren't just buying clothes; they were investing in narratives, in dreams spun from fabric.

But it wasn't just the fashion line that thrived. George and Taha, through their countless interactions, had built a partnership based on mutual respect and admiration. They challenged each other, drawing out the best in one another, their union of minds leading to unprecedented success.

Their story was a testament to the power of collaboration, of looking beyond conventional boundaries to find connections. It was a celebration of two minds, from different worlds, uniting to create magic. In the end, it wasn't just about fashion or business success; it was about the beauty that emerges when two souls truly understand and complement each other.

⚜

THE NEW DAWN

The darkness before dawn is often the most profound. A time when the world is still, shadows merging with the remaining vestiges of night. But as the horizon begins to paint its first streaks of colour, hope emerges, casting away the weight of the preceding hours, signalling a new beginning.

For George Miller, the preceding months had been tumultuous. An empire on the brink of collapse, a chance encounter, and a whirlwind journey of transformation— all had reshaped not just his business but his very understanding of life. Taha's entrance into his life was like the first rays of dawn, dispelling the gloom and bringing clarity.

The changes instituted under Taha's guidance had not only halted the decline of his empire but had ushered in a new era of prosperity. The brand's resurgence was apparent everywhere: from magazine covers lauding its innovative approach to customers wearing their products with pride. They weren't just wearing clothing; they were embodying a philosophy, a movement that intertwined sustainability, modernity, and deeply-rooted stories.

The headquarters, which once echoed with tense discussions and grim projections, now resounded with creativity and collaboration. The walls showcased success stories, testimonials from customers who felt seen and heard, and designs that resonated with their personal narratives. Workshops were frequently organized, where teams across departments would come together to understand global trends, ecological impacts, and most importantly, the shifting sands of consumer behavior.

Amidst this, George and Taha's relationship flourished. From professional consultations to deep, personal conversations late into the night, they had woven a bond that transcended conventional labels. Their combined vision for the company was now a shared dream, and their synergy was palpable.

One evening, as the sun painted the city in shades of gold, George stood by the vast windows of his office, lost in thought. Taha, having wrapped up a meeting, joined him. They stood side by side, watching the bustling city below—a city that was increasingly donning the fruits of their combined labor.

"Do you ever think about how we got here?" George mused, breaking the comfortable silence.

Taha smiled gently, "Every single day. But more than the 'how,' I think about the 'why.' Why the universe saw fit to make our paths cross, why out of all the challenges you faced, it was me—a woman of the night—who became the linchpin to change."

George looked at her, admiration clear in his eyes. "You were the wake-up call I needed. I was so entrenched in the old ways, in numbers and projections, that I'd forgotten the human element, the real essence of what makes a brand. And then you, with your wisdom, your lived experience, showed me a world I was blind to."

Taha chuckled, "You give me too much credit. All I did was show you a different perspective. The real work, the courage to change, that was all you."

He shook his head, "No, Taha. It was us. Together. I had the resources, and you had the insight. Our union, professional and personal, was what the company needed. What I needed."

They stood there, basking in the warmth of the setting sun and the journey they had embarked upon together. The city below seemed to move in a rhythmic dance—people returning home from work, children playing in parks, and cars gliding on roads. From this height, it all looked harmonious, peaceful.

The next day marked the grand opening of their flagship store after its redesign. As George and Taha entered, they were greeted by applause from their employees, stakeholders, and a few selected customers. The store was not just a commercial space but a testament to their new philosophy—a blend of culture, sustainability, and innovation.

The walls of the store were adorned with stories—of artisans who crafted the clothes, of communities that benefited from sustainable practices, and of customers who found a piece of themselves in the brand's collections.

Interactive screens allowed customers to trace the journey of each garment, right from its origin to the showroom.

The highlight of the store was the 'Heritage Section'—an idea birthed from Taha's narrative of understanding one's roots. It showcased traditional clothing from various cultures, each piece accompanied by its history and significance.

The event was a massive success, but for George and Taha, it was a moment of reflection. As they walked, admiring their work, they were approached by a young woman. Tears in her eyes, she said, "Thank you. In this piece," she gestured to a traditional dress, "I see my grandmother. I see my history. I never thought a global brand would make me feel this seen."

Taha squeezed George's hand. This was their impact. This was their new dawn.

Days turned into weeks, and the brand's influence grew not just as a fashion mogul but as a storyteller, a preserver of cultures, and a beacon of innovation. The blend of Taha's ground-level insights and George's expansive vision had breathed life into a brand that once teetered on the brink of oblivion.

And as each day dawned, it wasn't just about sales or market shares. It was about stories, connections, and making a difference—one garment, one story at a time.

ॐ

$\mathcal{L}$OVE $\mathcal{B}$EYOND $\mathcal{B}$OUNDARIES

$\mathcal{T}$aha's transformation had been meteoric. Her insights, untouched by corporate veils, had become integral in reviving the crumbling empire. With every passing day, her presence in the corporate fortress grew more pronounced. But beyond the corporate maze, another transformation, more profound and personal, was underway. The relationship between Taha and George was evolving, blurring lines and challenging conventions.

It began subtly, a lingering glance here, a soft touch there. The late-night strategy discussions often meandered into personal anecdotes, gradually painting the canvas of their pasts. In these moments, Taha and George, the corporate magnate and the street-smart survivor, disappeared. They became just George and Taha, two souls stripped of their labels, discovering the vulnerabilities and strengths that made them uniquely human.

One evening, after a particularly gruelling meeting, George invited Taha to his penthouse. "A change of scenery," he'd said. Even though Taha had visited Georges house a few times earlier, this time as she stepped in she was taken aback not by the opulence but by the sheer loneliness that the vast space echoed. She realized, beneath the armour of success, George was just a man searching for a connection.

They settled on the balcony, the city lights painting a serene backdrop. The night was alive with possibilities. George poured wine, and as the liquid shimmered in their glasses, the barriers began to melt.

"I often wonder," George began, his voice a whisper, "how different life would have been if our paths hadn't crossed. You've changed the trajectory of my empire. But more than that, you've touched a part of me that I had locked away."

Taha looked into his eyes, the intensity of his words weighing on her heart. "You saw me George, not as a commodity or a project, but as a person. You believed in me when the world only saw a label. That means more to me than you can imagine."

The hours rolled on as they delved deeper into their stories. With every meeting, Taha spoke more of certain aspects of her childhood, of dreams that were stolen too soon, and choices made of sheer necessity. Similarly, George also shared interesting and unknown tales of his rise, the weight of expectations, and the isolation that often accompanies success. Their stories, though worlds apart, had a common thread – a longing for genuine connection and understanding.

The night took a turn when George, hesitatingly, held out a small velvet box. Taha's breath caught in her throat as he opened it, revealing a delicate silver necklace with a pendant in the shape of two intertwined hands. "This," he murmured, "represents us. Two worlds, two lives, intertwined by fate."

Taha was overwhelmed, tears pooling in her eyes. She let George clasp the necklace around her neck, the cold metal a stark contrast to the warmth spreading through her heart.

Over the next few weeks, their bond deepened. They explored the city together, finding hidden gems in familiar landscapes. They danced under the stars, laughed at shared secrets, and held each other through silent tears. Their love story was unconventional, a tale of two people from opposite worlds finding solace in each other's arms.

But love, especially one that challenges societal norms, is rarely easy. Rumors began to swirl within the company corridors. Whispers of their relationship reached the tabloids, painting a sensational narrative. They faced criticism, both from the corporate world and from Taha's past acquaintances. Their love was scrutinized, labeled, and dissected.

One evening, as the weight of the world bore down on them, Taha turned to George. "Do you ever regret it? Letting me in, risking your reputation?"

George pulled her close, his voice firm. "Love is not defined by societal standards or boundaries. It's a connection, raw and pure. You, Taha, are my love story, a tale I'd choose over and over again."

Their journey was a testament to the power of love, proving that true connection goes beyond backgrounds and circumstances. They faced challenges, braved storms, but their love emerged stronger, a beacon for all those who dared to love beyond boundaries.

ॐ

SHAPING MINDS

The ripples of change initiated by George and Taha weren't confined to the walls of their stores or the pages of their catalogs. It extended far beyond, into communities, into conversations, and into classrooms.

Universities started developing case studies on the brand's resurgence, focusing on the amalgamation of grassroots wisdom and modern-day business strategies. The story of a magnate and a street-savvy woman became a popular topic of lectures, workshops, and seminars. Business schools around the world invited them to share their journey, aiming to inspire the next generation of leaders.

One such invitation took them to a well known Business School. As George stood behind the podium, looking at the sea of eager faces, he took a deep breath, glancing towards Taha, who sat among the audience, her ever-supportive presence reassuring him.

"Good evening, everyone," he began, his voice echoing through the hall. "Today, I stand before you not as the owner of a billion-dollar empire but as a student. A student of life, who was taught some of the most valuable lessons not in boardrooms or strategy meetings but on the streets, amidst the raw realities of life."

He narrated their story, of a chance encounter, of listening to and understanding a perspective so different from his own, and of the magic that ensued when they decided to bridge two worlds. Taha's insights into human behavior, her deep understanding of needs, desires, and emotions, and her ability to connect on a personal level were what the brand had been missing.

As he spoke of their challenges, their triumphs, and their vision for the future, the audience hung on to every word. The applause that followed was thunderous, but what moved George the most were the students who approached him afterward, expressing their admiration, their inspiration, and their desire to make a difference in their own unique ways.

The journey back to the hotel was one filled with contemplation. "Do you realize," Taha whispered, "that we're not just building a brand, but we're shaping thoughts, influencing minds, and perhaps even changing the course of how business will be perceived in the future?"

George smiled, pulling her close. "Yes, and to think this all began with one late-night conversation in a dimly-lit room."

Days swiftly transitioned into weeks, and their influence continued to grow. They launched initiatives to empower underprivileged women, offering them training, employment, and most importantly, respect and dignity. Artisans from remote villages were brought to the limelight, their crafts showcased on global platforms.

The media loved them. Interviews, cover stories, and documentaries—everyone wanted a piece of their tale. But amidst the glare of the spotlight, their bond grew stronger. They were not just business partners; they were confidantes, friends, and lovers, seamlessly moving between these roles.

One evening, as they walked on the beach, the setting sun casting a golden hue over the waters, George stopped, turning to face Taha. Taking a deep breath, he said, "I've seen many sunrises and sunsets, but none as beautiful as the new dawn you brought into my life. I want every sunrise, every new beginning, to be with you."

Kneeling on the sand, he produced a ring, its diamond glistening in the twilight. "Taha, will you marry me?"

Her eyes filled with tears, and with a nod and a choked voice, she whispered, "Yes."

And as the sun dipped below the horizon, their silhouettes merged into one, heralding not just another day, but a lifetime of new dawns, together.

❧

MARRIAGE

The days that followed were a whirlwind of emotions and preparations. While their professional lives had always been in the spotlight, their personal journey had been a more private affair. Now, with the news of their impending nuptials, the media had yet another sensational story. Yet, amidst the frenzied excitement, George and Taha remained a beacon of tranquillity, drawing strength from each other.

They decided on a simple wedding, surrounded by close friends and family. Yet, simple did not mean it lacked depth or significance. Every element of the ceremony was chosen with care, reflecting their shared values and experiences.

The venue was one of George's revamped showrooms, transformed into a haven of lights, flowers, and intimate spaces. Photos of their journey together adorned the walls: from that fateful night to their adventures across the world, and their combined efforts in revitalizing the company.

As Taha walked down the aisle, the room was enveloped in a hushed reverence. She looked radiant, her dress a collaborative creation, blending designs from the brand's artisans and her personal touch. It wasn't just a garment; it was a confluence of stories, dreams, and love. George, waiting at the altar, was struck by the weight of the moment. All his life's achievements seemed insignificant compared to the happiness of this instant.

The vows were deeply personal. George spoke of his gratitude, "Taha, you illuminated the darkest corners of my life, taught me humility, and showed me the boundless realms of love. I promise to learn from you every day, to laugh with you, to face challenges hand in hand, and to cherish our bond above all."

Taha's voice was soft but unwavering, "George, our paths crossed in the most unexpected of ways. You saw beyond the exterior, recognizing the soul beneath. You not only embraced my past but celebrated it. I vow to stand by you, to dream with you, and to nurture our love through every twist and turn."

As they exchanged rings, the atmosphere was electric, every heart in the room pulsating in harmony with theirs. The festivities that followed were joyous, with music, dance, and stories shared late into the night.

But, as with every story, challenges awaited. Their union, while celebrated by many, was not universally accepted. Critics questioned Taha's motives, while others cast aspersions on George's judgment. The business world speculated on how their personal relationship might impact the company.

The couple, however, remained undeterred. They continued their work with fervour, ensuring the brand's trajectory remained upward. Their bond was their greatest strength. Together, they faced scepticism, tackled challenges head-on, and silenced critics not with words but with undeniable results.

The sun rose and set, and, subtly, onths turned into years, and the couple's legacy grew. They expanded their empowerment initiatives, providing education, healthcare, and employment opportunities to marginalized communities. They also championed sustainable fashion, ensuring the brand was both profitable and environmentally responsible.

Their love story, while starting under unconventional circumstances, became a beacon of hope for many. It shattered stereotypes, questioned societal norms, and proved that love could be the most potent force of change.

MOVEMENT

As the seasons changed, so did the landscape of the fashion world. The brand that George and Taha had revitalized was no longer just a commercial entity; it had become a movement. A movement that stood for sustainable practices, for breaking societal norms, and for giving second chances to those who least expected it.

Their personal journey, intertwined with their professional resurgence, was a story taught in business schools and discussed in hushed tones in fashion circles. It was a narrative that showcased how, sometimes, the most unconventional pairings could lead to the most harmonious results.

One evening, as they sat in their penthouse overlooking the city that had been the backdrop to so much of their story, George turned to Taha, a contemplative look in his eyes. "Did you ever think," he began, pausing to find the right words, "that our story would be this... influential?"

Taha, with her ever-present wisdom, replied, "I knew our story was unique, but it's the sincerity and love we poured into everything that made it resonate with so many. Our story is not just ours; it's the story of every underdog, every person who has been judged without being understood, and every individual who dared to dream beyond societal confines."

Their annual gala was around the corner, an event that celebrated not only the brand's milestones but also the social initiatives they had undertaken. This year, the event was even more special. They were launching a foundation dedicated to providing education and vocational training to women in vulnerable situations, helping them reintegrate into society and find dignified work.

The night of the gala was a reflection of their journey together. The venue shimmered under a canopy of lights, each table adorned with photographs capturing pivotal moments from the past years. As guests arrived, they were greeted by an art installation at the entrance—a phoenix rising from the ashes, symbolizing rebirth, resilience, and resurgence.

The highlight of the evening was Taha's speech. As she took to the stage, the room was enveloped in a palpable silence, every pair of eyes fixed on her. She began, "Many of you know our story, but tonight isn't about us. It's about the countless women out there, much like myself, who find themselves in situations they didn't choose, judged by a world that doesn't understand them. Through our foundation, we aim to provide these women with the tools, education, and support they need to rebuild their lives."

She went on, her words eloquent and touching, recounting stories of women they had already helped and their aspirations for the foundation's future. The audience was moved, many to tears, as Taha's authenticity shone through.

As the evening wound down, and guests began to depart, the couple took a moment to themselves, reflecting on the journey that had brought them here. From a chance encounter to building a legacy that would impact generations.

In the years that followed, their foundation grew exponentially, touching the lives of thousands of women globally. George and Taha's love story, as improbable as it seemed, became a testament to the idea that love knows no bounds, that redemption is possible for anyone, and that sometimes, the most unexpected encounters can lead to the most profound transformations.

And so, in the annals of time, amidst tales of corporate success and legendary love stories, the tale of George and Taha would always stand out—

A story of love, resilience, and the power of second chances.

A tale of two worlds, two lives, intertwined by fate.

Your Ratings and Review Matter

Now that you have completed reading the book, I ask you kindly to go ahead and give your valuable rating and review.

If this book was useful to you and you were able to learn something new, or you were able to apply some of the techniques successfully, or you liked anything about this book, then my humble request is that you write a review so that it can help and benefit future readers.

I want to change the world through words and communication. I need your help to reach out to as many people as possible.

For an author, there is no greater and better return than a testimonial.

Also, if you want to contact the author or give any kind of feedback, please feel free to write to connect@vishal-gupta.com

ACKNOWLEDGMENTS

We cannot do everything ourselves. We all need relatives, friends, and well-wishers, who support us and believe in us. I thank, from the bottom of my heart, all the people mentioned below for supporting me, believing in me, and for giving their precious time to me so that I could give the best to this book.

THANK YOU!

(Alphabetically) Aalok Mehta, Alka Sooden, Aniket Phule, AnilAgarwal (Dr.), Anoop Pandey, Chetan Bansal, Deepa Shah,Dilip Ahuja, Ibrahim Bohra, Jiya Gupta, Krati Gupta, Prabodh Agarwal, Reena Rupani, Saurabh Jain, Samir Agarwal, Satyajit Fovkar, Shashank Shah,Siddhanth Jain, Som Bathla, Sudhanshu Garg, Swati Gupta, Vyom Gupta.

Cover Concept & Design by CREATIVE PLANET : creativeplanetinc@gmail.com

DEDICATION

This book is devoted to Shri Satish Malhotra of Empire Industries, who afforded me the opportunity to spearhead premier fashion courses in India. I will forever be grateful to him for the confidence he placed in me, a luxury not many would have afforded to a 30-year-old. His faith was a beacon of support during times when belief in my capabilities was scarce.

DISCLAIMER

Although the publisher and the author have made every effort to ensure that the information in this book was correct at press time and while this publication is designed to provide accurate information regarding the subject matter covered, the publisher and the author assume no responsibility for errors, inaccuracies, omissions, or any other inconsistencies herein and hereby disclaim any liability to any party for any loss, damage, or disruption caused by errors or omissions, whether such errors or omissions result from negligence, accident, or any other cause.

The ideas, procedures, and suggestions contained in this book are not intended as a substitute for consulting with an expert.

Neither the author nor the publisher shall be liable or responsible for any loss or damage allegedly arising from any information or suggestion in this book.

Names, characters, and incidents in this book are either the products of the author's imagination or used in a fictitious manner. Any resemblance to an actual person, living or dead, or actual events is purely coincidental.

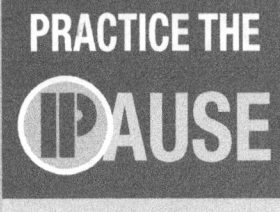

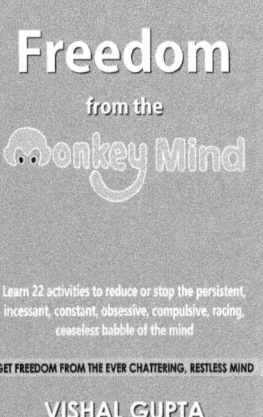

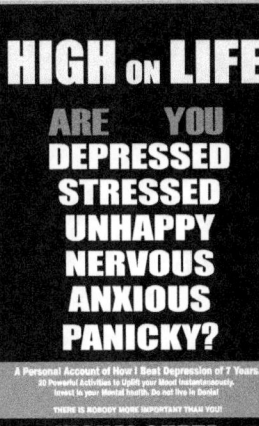

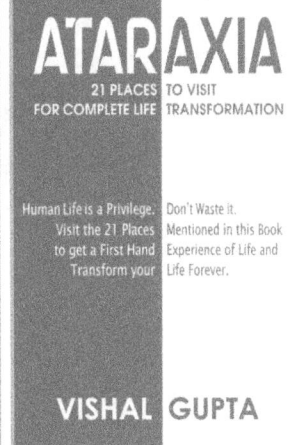

www.vishal-gupta.com/amazon-page